THE EVOLUTION
OF AFRICA'S MAJOR NATIONS

Tanzania

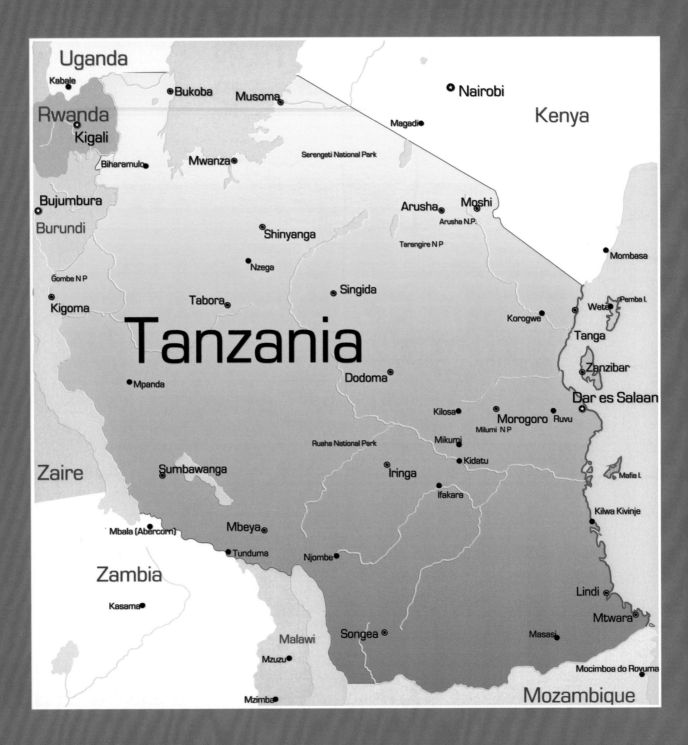

THE EVOLUTION
OF AFRICA'S MAJOR NATIONS

Tanzania

Joan Vos MacDonald

Mason Crest
Philadelphia

Mason Crest
370 Reed Road
Broomall, PA 19008
www.masoncrest.com

CPSIA Compliance Information: Batch #EAMN2013-24. For further information,
contact Mason Crest at 1-866-MCP-Book.

First printing

1 3 5 7 9 8 6 4 2

Library of Congress Cataloging-in-Publication Data

MacDonald, Joan Vos.
  Tanzania / Joan Vos MacDonald.
     p. cm. — (The evolution of Africa's major nations.)
  Includes bibliographical references and index.
  ISBN 978-1-4222-2186-0 (hardcover)
  ISBN 978-1-4222-2214-0 (pbk.)
  ISBN 978-1-4222-9427-7 (ebook)
  1. Tanzania—Juvenile literature. I. Title. II. Series: Evolution of Africa's major nations.
  DT438.M252 2011
  967.8—dc22
                            2010048002

Africa: Facts and Figures	Egypt	Nigeria
The African Union	Ethiopia	Rwanda
Algeria	Ghana	Senegal
Angola	Ivory Coast	Sierra Leone
Botswana	Kenya	South Africa
Burundi	Liberia	Sudan
Cameroon	Libya	Tanzania
Democratic Republic	Morocco	Uganda
of the Congo	Mozambique	Zimbabwe

Table of Contents

Introduction   6
Robert I. Rotberg

A Dramatic Landscape   11

Land of Two Histories   21

Two Nations Work Together   39

The Economy: Gains and Setbacks   47

The People of Tanzania   57

Along the Caravan Route and the Coast   67

A Calendar of Tanzanian Festivals   74

Recipes   76

Glossary   78

Project and Report Ideas   80

Chronology   82

Further Reading/Internet Resources   84

For More Information   85

Index   86

Africa: Progress, Problems, and Promise

Robert I. Rotberg

Africa is the cradle of humankind, but for millennia it was off the familiar, beaten path of global commerce and discovery. Its many peoples therefore developed largely apart from the diffusion of modern knowledge and the spread of technological innovation until the 17th through 19th centuries. With the coming to Africa of the book, the wheel, the hoe, and the modern rifle and cannon, foreigners also brought the vastly destructive transatlantic slave trade, oppression, discrimination, and onerous colonial rule. Emerging from that crucible of European rule, Africans created nationalistic movements and then claimed their numerous national independences in the 1960s. The result is the world's largest continental assembly of new countries.

There are 53 members of the African Union, a regional political grouping, and 48 of those nations lie south of the Sahara. Fifteen of them, including mighty Ethiopia, are landlocked, making international trade and economic growth that much more arduous and expensive. Access to navigable rivers is limited, natural harbors are few, soils are poor and thin, several countries largely consist of miles and miles of sand, and tropical diseases have sapped the strength and productivity of innumerable millions. Being landlocked, having few resources (although countries along Africa's west coast have tapped into deep offshore petroleum and gas reservoirs), and being beset by malaria, tuberculosis, schistosomiasis, AIDS, and many other maladies has kept much of Africa poor for centuries.

Thirty-two of the world's poorest 44 countries are African. Hunger is common. So is rapid deforestation and desertification. Unemployment rates are often over 50 percent, for jobs are few—even in agriculture. Where Africa once

Wildebeests grazw near Tarangire River, Tarangire National Park.

was a land of small villages and a few large cities, with almost everyone engaged in growing grain or root crops or grazing cattle, camels, sheep, and goats, today more than half of all the more than 1 billion Africans, especially those who live south of the Sahara, reside in towns and cities. Traditional agriculture hardly pays, and a number of countries in Africa—particularly the smaller and more fragile ones—can no longer feed themselves.

There is not one Africa, for the continent is full of contradictions and variety. Of the 750 million people living south of the Sahara, at least 150 million live in Nigeria, 85 million in Ethiopia, 68 million in the Democratic Republic of the Congo, and 49 million in South Africa. By contrast, tiny Djibouti and Equatorial Guinea have fewer than 1 million people each, and prosperous

Detail from a slavery memorial on Zanzibar. The Indian Ocean island was a major center of the slave trade in East Africa until the late 19th century.

Botswana and Namibia each are under 2.2 million in population. Within some countries, even medium-sized ones like Zambia (12 million), there are a plethora of distinct ethnic groups speaking separate languages. Zambia, typical with its multitude of competing entities, has 70 such peoples, roughly broken down into four language and cultural zones. Three of those languages jostle with English for primacy.

Given the kaleidoscopic quality of African culture and deep-grained poverty, it is no wonder that Africa has developed economically and politically less rapidly than other regions. Since independence from colonial rule, weak governance has also plagued Africa and contributed significantly to the widespread poverty of its peoples. Only Botswana and offshore Mauritius have been governed democratically without interruption since independence. Both are among Africa's wealthiest countries, too, thanks to the steady application of good governance.

Aside from those two nations, and South Africa, Africa has been a continent of coups since 1960, with massive and oil-rich Nigeria suffering incessant periods of harsh, corrupt, autocratic military rule. Nearly every other country on or around the continent, small and large, has been plagued by similar bouts of instability and dictatorial rule. In the 1970s and 1980s Idi Amin ruled Uganda capriciously and Jean-Bedel Bokassa proclaimed himself emperor of the Central African Republic. Macias Nguema of Equatorial Guinea was another in that same mold. More recently Daniel arap Moi held Kenya in thrall and Robert Mugabe has imposed himself on once-prosperous Zimbabwe. In both of those cases, as in the case of Gnassingbe Eyadema in Togo and the late Mobutu Sese Seko in Congo, these presidents stole wildly and drove entire peoples and their nations into penury. Corruption is common in Africa, and so are a weak rule-of-law framework, misplaced development, high expenditures on soldiers and low expenditures on health and education, and a widespread (but not universal) refusal on the part of leaders to work well for their followers and citizens.

Conflict between groups within countries has also been common in Africa. More than 12 million Africans have been killed in civil wars since 1990, while another 9 million have become refugees. Decades of conflict in Sudan led to a January 2011 referendum in which the people of southern Sudan voted overwhelmingly to secede and form a new state. In early 2011, anti-government protests spread throughout North Africa, ultimately toppling long-standing regimes in Tunisia and Egypt. That same year, there were serious ongoing hostilities within Chad, Ivory Coast, Libya, the Niger Delta region of Nigeria, and Somalia.

Despite such dangers, despotism, and decay, Africa is improving. Botswana and Mauritius, now joined by South Africa, Senegal, Kenya, and Ghana, are beacons of democratic growth and enlightened rule. Uganda and Senegal are taking the lead in combating and reducing the spread of AIDS, and others are following. There are serious signs of the kinds of progressive economic policy changes that might lead to prosperity for more of Africa's peoples. The trajectory in Africa is positive.

(Opposite) Mount Kilimanjaro, located in northeastern Tanzania, is Africa's highest peak. (Right) Traditional fishing boats on a beach at Pemba Island, part of the Zanzibar archipelago. The island is located in the Indian Ocean about 31 miles (50 km) east of mainland Tanzania, across a stretch of water known as the Pemba Channel.

A Dramatic Landscape

KARIBU! THAT'S THE word for welcome in Swahili, the national language of the United Republic of Tanzania. This land of many wonders welcomes visitors and invites them to explore its breathtakingly beautiful terrain. Tanzania has majestic mountains (including Africa's tallest peak), large volcanic craters, immense lakes, huge areas of undeveloped wilderness, and a vast diversity of wildlife.

Most of the territory in the United Republic of Tanzania lies on the mainland of Africa; this part of the country is known as Tanganyika. A handful of islands in the Indian Ocean make up the rest of Tanzania; collectively they are called the Zanzibar islands.

Tanzania, located just south of the equator, is the largest country in East Africa, with an area of 364,803 square miles (945,087 square kilometers). It is bordered by Kenya and Uganda to the north; by Burundi, Rwanda, the Democratic Republic of the Congo, and Zambia to the west; and by Malawi and Mozambique to the south. Tanzania's coastline along the Indian Ocean runs about 885 miles (1,425 kilometers).

Tanzania has more inland water—over 22,700 square miles (59,000 sq km)—than any other African country. Most of this water is contained in lakes located in the long geological depression known as the Great Rift Valley.

A giraffe stands on the Serengeti in Tanzania. Giraffes, the world's tallest animal, can reach 19 feet (5.8 meters) in height. Today, Serengeti National Park is a world-famous wildlife preserve that is home to huge herds of wildebeest, zebras, gazelles, elands, and giraffes, lions, and other animals.

GEOGRAPHIC REGIONS AND FEATURES

The mainland of Tanzania can be divided into three types of terrain: plains, located along the coast; highlands in the north and south; and a central *plateau*. Vegetation varies considerably, in some cases within fairly small areas. Tanzania is home to savanna (a grassland with no trees or only scattered trees), woodland with leaf-shedding trees, lowland rain forest, evergreen forest, highland desert, heath, and *moorland*.

The central plateau, which makes up most of the country, is primarily grasslands with some mountains. At a height of about 1,200 feet (366 meters) above sea level, the plateau is bordered by Lake Victoria to the north, the Rukwa Valley to the south, Lake Tanganyika and the Ruwenzori Mountains to the west, and the coastal plains to the east. The central plateau includes the Serengeti Plain and the Masai Steppe.

The mountainous northeastern region is home to the fabled Mount Kilimanjaro, Africa's highest point at 19,341 feet (5,895 meters) above sea level, and Mount Meru, which rises to a height of 14,954 feet (4,558 meters). A favorite among mountaineers, Kilimanjaro is the most awe-inspiring mountain on the continent. It can take a week to climb, and on the ascent hikers travel through tropical forest, moorland, alpine desert, and ice fields. Mount Meru, Africa's fifth-highest peak, is a three- or four-day hike. On their way to the top, hikers travel through plains, forest, and a lava desert.

To the west of these famous peaks is the Serengeti National Park, one of the world's best-known wildlife preserves. The park, roughly the size of the state of Connecticut, is home to at least 35 species of savanna-dwelling animals. Its vast treeless plains are a favorite destination for safaris. In fact, the word *safari* is derived from a Swahili word for journey.

To the south of the Serengeti National Park is the Ngorongoro Crater Conservation Area, a place of dramatic landscapes, including the volcanic crater from which the reserve takes its name. Ngorongoro also contains Olduvai Gorge, a canyon that is approximately 328 feet (100 meters) deep and runs for about 30 miles (48 km). The gorge has yielded a rich fossil record, including many of the earliest known **hominid** bones. Discoveries at Olduvai revolutionized scientists' understanding of the first human species. It was here that Professor Louis Leakey and his wife, Mary, uncovered a 1.7-million-year-old hominid jawbone in 1959. Other fossil finds at Olduvai during the 1960s—hominid bones as well as primitive stone tools—were slightly older and led Louis Leakey to suggest that a species named *Homo habilis* was the first human species.

West of the Serengeti is Lake Victoria, Africa's largest freshwater lake. It covers an area of 26,873 square miles (69,484 sq km) but is only about 276 feet (84 meters) at its deepest. Lake Victoria is the source of the Nile River.

Southwest of Lake Victoria is Lake Tanganyika, the world's longest freshwater lake. It is also one of the world's oldest lakes, having been formed some 20 million years ago, and is the second-deepest lake in Africa, plunging to depths of 4,823 feet (1,470 meters).

Near Lake Tanganyika is Gombe National Park, where Jane Goodall's chimpanzee research station is located. Through years of painstaking observation, Goodall made important discoveries about chimpanzee behavior, including the way humans' closest animal relatives use tools. In the process, she helped change accepted theories about what differentiates humans from other mammals.

Lake Malawi (also called Lake Nyasa), the third-largest lake on the continent, lies southeast of Lake Tanganyika in another mountainous region. East of Lake Malawi is the Selous Game Reserve. Covering an area the size

Lake Victoria, Africa's largest freshwater lake, is the source of the Nile River.

of Switzerland, it is the largest game reserve in Africa and is home to more than 50,000 elephants, 440 species of birds, and the rare and protected African hunting dog.

THE ISLANDS

The name Zanzibar applies to the Zanzibar *archipelago* and includes Zanzibar Island (also known as Unguja), Pemba Island, Tumbatu Island, and several smaller islands, such as Chapwani, Bawe, Chumbe, Chunguu, and Mnemba. The islands were once known for the valuable spices grown there,

THE GEOGRAPHY OF TANZANIA

Location: Eastern Africa, bordering the Indian Ocean, between Kenya and Mozambique

Area: slightly larger than twice the size of California;
   total: 365,755 square miles (947,300 sq km; includes the islands of Mafia, Pemba, and Zanzibar)
   land: 342,009 square miles (885,800 sq km)
   water: 23,745 square miles (61,500 sq km)

Borders: Burundi, 280 miles (451 km); Democratic Republic of the Congo, 285 miles (459 km); Kenya, 478 miles (769 km); Malawi, 295 miles (475 km); Mozambique, 470 miles (756 km); Rwanda, 135 miles (217 km); Uganda, 246 miles (396 km); Zambia, 210 miles (338 km)

Climate: varies from tropical along coast to temperate in highlands

Terrain: plains along coast; central plateau; highlands in north and south

Elevation extremes:
   lowest point: Indian Ocean, 0 feet
   highest point: Kilimanjaro, 19,341 feet (5,895 meters)

Natural hazards: flooding on the central plateau during the rainy season; drought; limited volcanic activity.

Source: CIA World Factbook, 2011.

and even today a number of plantations remain, filling the air with the fragrant scent of cloves, cinnamon, nutmeg, and vanilla.

Zanzibar is a popular vacation destination, attracting visitors with its white sandy beaches fringed with coconut trees, banana palms, and mangroves; its coral reefs; and its warm, translucent waters, which teem with sea life. In fact, the waters around the Zanzibar islands boast four times the sea life found in the Caribbean, which makes them a favorite destination for divers. Most popular is the green island of Pemba, once known as "the Pearl of the Ocean."

The main island—Zanzibar or Unguja Island—has been a popular port for centuries, drawing waves of traders, explorers, and adventurers from many cultures. Among the most influential were the *Shirazi* Persians and the Omani Arabs, and their culture and architecture became dominant. In 2000 the United Nations Educational, Scientific and Cultural Organization (UNESCO) designated Stone Town—the old section of the capital, Zanzibar City—a World Heritage site.

A VARIED CLIMATE

Tanzania's climate varies by region, though the country's proximity to the equator means that seasonal variations are minimal. Along the coast and on the offshore islands, tropical conditions prevail. Average daytime temperatures are about 81° Fahrenheit (27° Celsius) during the summer months (December to March), and 73°F (23°C) during the winter (June to September). Humidity can be high, though the area does enjoy cool sea breezes. Average annual rainfall exceeds 40 inches (102 centimeters).

The central plateau is dry to arid, with average annual rainfall of only about 10 inches (25 cm). High temperatures may reach 80°F (27°C) from June through August, and 86°F (30°C) between December and March.

The highlands of the northeast and southwest are cool and temperate. Temperatures reach around 68°F (20°C) during the day and may drop below 59°F (15°C) during the nights. Temperatures can remain below freezing year-round on top of ice-capped Mount Kilimanjaro.

During Tanzania's rainy season, torrential downpours may occur for days on end in certain areas of the country. On the coast, the rainy season lasts from March to June. In the highlands, there are two rainy seasons: from November to December and February to May. Heavy downpours may endanger land in the central plateau. Flooding is a regular problem, and the erosion of good soil from farmable land is a long-term issue. Yet despite the seasonal rains, drought may be a problem at various times of the year, especially in the naturally drier regions.

WILDLIFE IN TANZANIA

With one-quarter of its land dedicated to national parks and game reserves, Tanzania boasts a greater percentage of protected wildlife areas than any other country in the world. More than 300 species of animals are native to Tanzania, at least 30 of which are considered endangered.

Mainland Tanganyika is home to the chimpanzee, zebra, eland, reedbuck, lion, elephant, black rhino, wart hog, hippopotamus, golden jackal, black-backed jackal, bat-eared fox, Thompson's gazelle, and wildebeest. The Zanzibar islands are home to monkeys, bush pigs, small antelopes, and African civets. Various species of mongoose can also be found there. The

Hippos in the Ngorongoro Crater Conservation Area, located in northern Tanzania.

multitude of animals in Tanzania, many in danger of extinction, make the country a popular destination for tourists and nature photographers.

One favorite animal attraction for visitors—and also for nearby lions—is the annual wildebeest migration across the Grumeti River. In May or June, when the grass they eat becomes scarce, as many as 1.5 million wildebeests (also known as gnus) move west and north in search of food.

Besides the various species of plain-dwelling wildlife, Tanzania is also known for the rich diversity of its bird life. In January and February, thousands of flamingos descend like a rosy haze on Ngorongoro Crater and Lake Magdi. The Wembere Swamps in western Tanzania are a breeding ground for wading birds such as herons, ibises, and storks. Katavi National Park in western Tanzania hosts large flocks of pelicans, while the Uwanda Game Reserve is home to gray parrots and woodpeckers.

(Opposite) Jakaya Mrisho Kikwete, president of the United Republic of Tanzania (right), chats with United Nations Secretary-General Ban Ki-moon during a 2011 meeting of the African Leaders' Malaria Alliance. (Right) The Old Fort in Stone Town, Zanzibar, was built around 1700 by an Omani sultan. The island was ruled by Oman for more than 200 years.

2 Land of Two Histories

THE HISTORY OF Tanzania is actually two histories—the history of inland Tanganyika and the story of Zanzibar and the coast. It was only during the second half of the 20th century that the two regions merged into a national alliance.

Archaeologists have uncovered clues to the ancient history of inland Tanganyika in the tools and fossils found in excavations there. Prehistoric footprints found in and near the Olduvai Gorge suggest that some of our earliest human ancestors lived there more than 3 million years ago.

It is also believed that more than 5,000 years ago, the interior area of Tanganyika was inhabited by tribes using a *click-tongue language* similar to that of southern Africa's Bushmen and Hottentot tribes. These hunter-gatherers were eventually displaced by successive migrations of other tribes that farmed and herded animals. The last inland migrations of tribes took place in the 19th century, and today there are as many as 130 different tribes in Tanzania.

People of ancient cultures were well acquainted with the region today known as Tanzania. Egyptian merchant ships first explored the east coast of Africa around 3000 B.C., and the ancient Greeks and Romans both recorded visits to an East African land called Azania, which was rich in ivory. Some historians believe Zanzibar may have been the location of the kingdom of Sheba (Saba), which is mentioned in the Old Testament of the Bible. Visitors came from the East as well: Arab, Persian, and Indian merchants visited both Zanzibar and the coast. They came to trade textiles, beads, and dye for local goods such as ivory, gold, rhino horns, tortoise shells, leopard skins, coconut oil, and *ambergris*.

Although Zanzibar itself had few resources, its position in the Indian Ocean made it a natural trade port. Omani Arabs visited the coast and Zanzibar for hundreds of years, and by the eighth century A.D. they had established settlements in both places. They intermarried with local tribespeople, merging Arab and *Bantu* cultures. The name Zanzibar comes from the Omani Arab *Zinj el Barr*, which means "land of the black people." At the time Zanzibar referred to the entire area of the eastern coast.

Around A.D. 750, groups of Muslims from Shiraz, Persia, migrated to the area, fleeing civil wars. They were known as the Shirazi. Persian followers of the ancient *Zoroastrian* faith also migrated to the area. The word for Tanzania's official language (Swahili) comes from the Persian word for coast (*sahel*). The Shirazi helped settle Kilwa Kisiwani, which by the 13th century had become one of the most prominent island trading ports in East Africa. Gold was traded at Kilwa Kisiwani, and gold coins were minted there.

Both the Omani and Shirazi settlers brought the Islamic faith with them. The first mosque in Tanzania was built in 830, and the practice of Islam was widespread in the coastal area by the 14th century.

EUROPEANS ARRIVE IN ZANZIBAR

By the 1200s, European countries had become interested in trading with Asian rulers for spices, silk, jade, and other products that were not available in Europe. The land route to Asia was long and dangerous, so goods from the East commanded high prices. The rulers of Portugal hoped to find a sea route east to Asia, by which they could acquire the goods more cheaply. Throughout the 15th century, Portuguese explorers charted a route south along the western coast of Africa.

Portuguese navigator Vasco da Gama stopped at Zanzibar in 1498, during his voyage around the Horn of Africa to India. Within a decade, Portugal controlled the coastal area of East Africa.

In 1497 the Portuguese explorer Vasco da Gama rounded the southern tip of Africa and became the first European explorer to reach the Indian Ocean. Da Gama sailed into Zanzibar while on his way to India, and he was impressed by the island's wealthy and sophisticated ports. In 1502 da Gama returned to visit Kilwa Kisiwani, then a city of beautiful palaces and mosques, some built with coral stone. His reports of island dwellers who wore silk and gems and possessed fine tapestries must have impressed Portuguese authorities. Later that year, another Portuguese adventurer, Francisco de Almeida, returned with an army to plunder Kilwa. By 1506 Portugal controlled the coast. Soon it was the dominant power in the region and controlled the Indian Ocean trade.

The Portuguese were not tolerant rulers, and life on the Zanzibar islands was often difficult and unsettled while they were in power. In 1698 the people of Zanzibar, with help from Omani Arabs, drove the Portuguese out of their country. The islands then fell under Omani control.

Under the rule of the *sultans* of Oman, cloves, Zanzibar's main export crop, were first planted. Caravans were organized to travel into the African mainland, and the slave trade, which dated back at least to the eighth century, began supplying greater numbers of captives to the slave market in Zanzibar. In 1841 the Omani sultan, Sayyid Said bin Sultan, moved the capital of his kingdom from Oman, on the Arabian Peninsula, to Zanzibar.

EXPLORING THE MAINLAND

During the 19th century, European missionaries and explorers visited inland Tanganyika and began to share its mysteries with the world. Among the most famous explorers of this time were Richard Burton, John Hanning Speke, David Livingstone, and Henry Morton Stanley. Burton and Speke journeyed to Africa in 1856 to find the source of the Nile River. In 1858 they arrived at Lake Tanganyika but determined that it was not the source of the Nile. Burton became too sick to continue on, but Speke persisted, and six months later he found the true source of the Nile: a large body of water he named Lake Victoria, in honor of the queen of England. Speke led a third expedition that explored the area around Lake Victoria in 1860.

Livingstone first traveled to Africa as a missionary but became interested in finding the source of the Zambezi River. During his eighth year in Africa, he became ill and lost touch with the outside world. Henry Morton Stanley, a reporter for the *New York Herald* newspaper, traveled to Africa to look for him. After a long search, Stanley heard stories about a white man liv-

Welsh-born explorer Henry Morton Stanley meets the Scottish missionary-explorer David Livingstone near Lake Tanganyika, 1871. Stanley went on to explore much of central Africa himself.

ing near Lake Tanganyika. The two explorers finally met in 1871, when Stanley uttered the famous line, "Dr. Livingstone, I presume." Within two years Livingstone, who had long been ill, died; Stanley went on to explore central Africa, later recounting his adventures in several books.

COLONIZATION

In the 19th century, European countries—competing with one another for natural resources to feed their expanding industries—penetrated the continent of Africa and established colonies. The Europeans frequently tried to paint their territorial expansions as morally good enterprises, claiming that they were bringing Christianity and civilization to Africa's "heathen savages."

During the late 1800s Germany and England both became interested in East Africa. Germany focused its attention on the mainland. In 1884 Karl Peters, who represented an organization called the German Colonization Society—which promoted German interests in underdeveloped countries—signed treaties with tribal chiefs in Tanganyika. The treaties offered the tribes protection from one another and from other European colonial powers. For their part, Germany

A coconut market in Tanganyika, circa 1936.

and Britain divided up the area with the Anglo-German Agreement of 1890, which gave Germany control of Tanganyika and Britain control of Zanzibar.

Although Germany introduced the cultivation of new crops and built roads and railroads throughout its colony, German policies of taxation, forced labor, and land confiscation bred resentment. Eventually this resulted in the Maji Maji Rebellion, which lasted from 1905 to 1907. During the rebellion many tribes united to fight the Germans. The Tanganyikan warriors believed that drinking sacred water known as *maji* would protect them from German bullets. It did not, and more than 120,000 people were killed before the Germans finally put down the rebellion. Although the Maji Maji uprising failed, the unity achieved by various Tanganyikan tribes would later be considered an important first step toward nationalism and independence.

On Zanzibar the Omani sultan would remain the nominal ruler, but he took his orders from a British official. When Khalid, the son of Sultan Barghash, proclaimed himself sultan against British wishes, Zanzibar became the site of the shortest war in recorded history. At 9:02 A.M. on August 27, 1896, three British warships opened fire on the palace complex. By 9:40 A.M., after two palaces had been reduced to rubble and 500 people killed, Khalid surrendered.

Like the Germans, the British introduced new practices and policies throughout Zanzibar. In 1897 British authorities abolished slavery on Zanzibar, closing the island's infamous slave market.

Germany and Britain found themselves on opposite sides when World War I broke out in August 1914. At the end of the four-year conflict, an international association of countries, the League of Nations, was created. The League gave control of the colonial territories of Germany and its defeated allies to Britain, France, and other countries. Britain received control over Tanganyika.

Under the League of Nations' mandate system, the British were supposed to prepare the territories they controlled for independence at some future date. Until then, however, Britain had what amounted to a free hand in how the territories were governed and how their natural resources were used.

The League of Nations had been created with the hope that an international assembly of nations could prevent future wars. Unfortunately, it proved to be ineffective. By the mid-1930s Japanese armies were invading mainland China, and Germany was again preparing for war. In 1939 the Second World War began with Germany's invasion of Poland. Tanganyika was far from the actual fighting, and its economy expanded dramatically because of demand for its natural resources. Revenue from overseas trade grew 600 percent between 1939 and 1949.

INDEPENDENCE

After the end of World War II, a new international organization, the United Nations, was formed to replace the League of Nations. In place of the mandate system, the U.N. established a system of trusteeships for the colonial territories, with the goal of helping them achieve self-government. Although the European powers would continue to administer the territories, the U.N. Trusteeship Council would oversee their movement toward independence. In 1946 Tanganyika became a U.N. trust territory under British administration.

An independence movement had existed in Tanganyika for decades. The strongest nationalist party was the Tanganyika African National Union

Celebrating Tanganyika's independence on December 9, 1961, a jubilant crowd carries aloft their country's leader, Julius Nyerere.

(TANU), which had been formed in 1929. From 1954 the party was led by Julius Nyerere, a former schoolteacher and graduate of the University of Edinburgh in Scotland. During elections in August 1960, TANU won all but one seat in the Tanganyika Legislative Council, and Nyerere became chief minister. In that capacity he led the country to independence, which was proclaimed on December 9, 1961. In 1962 the country adopted a constitution and Nyerere was reelected. The next year, Tanganyika became a *one-party state*.

Zanzibar became independent from British rule on December 10, 1963, with the formation of the Sultanate of Zanzibar. However, many of the island's inhabitants believed that the new government, which was dominated by Zanzibari Arabs, did not represent them. African resentment of the small but powerful Arab population grew until January 12, 1964, when the government was overthrown. The violent revolution culminated in the creation of the People's Republic of Zanzibar and Pemba, with Sheikh Abeid Amani Karume of the Afro-Shirazi Party becoming prime minister of the Revolutionary Council. Karume soon banned all other political parties and established relationships with communist countries such as Cuba and China, which sent engineers and offered other technical help to Zanzibar.

Karume wanted to share Zanzibar's wealth equally among its citizens and turn Zanzibar's palaces into housing facilities. However, his governing methods earned him accusations of human rights violations and brought him political enemies. To strengthen their respective positions, Nyerere invited Zanzibar to unite with Tanganyika to form the Republic of Tanzania. A union constitution, which let the islands maintain their own laws and government, was ratified on April 26, 1964. Nyerere became president and Karume became first vice president, a position he held until his assassination in April 1972. On February 6, 1977, TANU and the Afro-Shirazi Party merged into a single party called Chama Cha Mapinduzi, or CCM (Revolutionary Party).

THE POLICIES OF NYERERE

Julius Nyerere's vision for Tanzania was a nation whose people were not divided by tribe, race, or class but rather were unified by a common national identity and shared goals. Fulfilling that vision would be a formidable task. Instead of thinking of themselves as members of a specific cultural group or tribe—and there were about 130 distinct tribes in the country—the people would have to identify themselves first and foremost as Tanzanians.

One way to promote a sense of national identity, Nyerere decided, would be for all Tanzanians to speak the same language. Thus he made Swahili, also called Kiswahili, the country's official language. (In Zanzibar the name for the Swahili language is Kiunguju.) As a former teacher, Nyerere also believed that education could help create a sense of national identity, in addition to its vital role in laying the foundations for a better standard of living for Tanzania. Nyerere closed private schools, which had been run primarily by missionaries, and devoted government funds to establishing an effective public school system. He also made primary school attendance mandatory.

In many respects Nyerere's most ambitious—and most controversial— policy was the creation of small, socialist-inspired communal farming villages. He abolished tribal chiefdoms, asking people from the countryside to move into these collective *ujamma* ("togetherness") villages. The *ujamma* would supposedly reflect the traditional African values of "familyhood" and community and not be based on what Nyerere viewed as the exploitative and acquisitive values characteristic of capitalist systems. At first, from 1967 to 1973, Tanzanians did not have to move to these villages, and many resisted leaving their homes and their traditional ways of life for living arrangements dictated by the government. Eventually, however, government officials used more coercive measures—including, in some cases, the destruction of people's homes— in order to effect a massive transfer of the rural population to the *ujamma*. Unfortunately, the *ujamma* experiment was a dismal failure in economic terms: agricultural production tumbled, and the economy suffered greatly.

Nyerere's policies did result in some improvements, however. When he became president of Tanzania in 1964, the average life expectancy was 35 years, and just 15 percent of the population could read. By 1980 life expectancy averaged 45 years, 90 percent of the population could read, and access to

A Tanzanian woman cooks newly harvested yams at her rural home in a communal farming village, circa 1980. President Nyerere's socialist policies led to the uprooting of many Tanzanians, while not improving the standard of living for most people.

health care, clean water, and schools had been improved.

Critics insisted that these successes were overshadowed by the failure of the *ujamma* experiment and by the corrupt and inefficient one-party system Nyerere had championed. By the late 1970s Tanzania was forced to take international loans to feed its people. By 1980 the economic situation was so bad that food was rationed.

Involvement in conflicts in other African countries also had a negative effect on Tanzania. Nyerere supported wars for independence in Angola and Mozambique, as well as the overthrow of a minority white government in Rhodesia.

In 1978 neighboring Uganda, under the leadership of the dictator Idi Amin, invaded Tanzania's Kagera Region. Tanzania assembled an army of

50,000 men and, with the help of Ugandan exiles, not only drove back the well-trained Ugandan army, but also helped overthrow Amin's regime. Although this was considered a victory, the war left Tanzania even more dependent on international loans.

As a condition of receiving financial aid, Western governments and world financial organizations required Tanzania to make some social and economic reforms—such as allowing the formation of more political parties, giving citizens more rights, and transferring some government-run enterprises to the private sector. Tanzania's leaders decided to comply and began privatizing certain businesses. In 1984 the constitution was amended to include a bill of rights, along with provisions guaranteeing direct elections to the National Assembly, with seats set aside for women, labor union officials, and appointees.

Nyerere resigned in 1985 after serving four terms. His successor, President Ali Hassan Mwinyi, privatized more businesses, helped set up the first Tanzanian private bank, and encouraged foreign investment.

AIDS BECOMES A MAJOR PROBLEM

During the early 1980s, AIDS—a disease that attacks and destroys the human immune system—first appeared in Tanzania. It is believed that the disease spread into Tanzania from Uganda during the 1978–79 war; the first AIDS cases in Tanzania were diagnosed in 1983.

The disease has had devastating effects socially and economically. Today health officials estimate that nearly 10 percent of the people living in Tanzania's cities are infected with HIV, the virus that causes AIDS. The rate

In a Tanzanian hospital, a woman cares for her husband, who has AIDS. Like many communities of sub-Saharan Africa, Tanzania has been decimated by AIDS over the past three decades.

of infection in rural areas is much lower, although it is rising. Overall, 5.6 percent of Tanzanian adults have AIDS or are infected with HIV, according to a 2009 estimate by the United Nations.

Tanzania's children, too, are suffering greatly as a result of the epidemic. Some 200,000 Tanzanian children under age 15 are infected with HIV. In addition, 1.3 million Tanzanian children have lost one or both parents to AIDS, according to United Nations estimates. Given the high rates of infection in the country, that number is likely to continue to rise. Many of these orphans have few if any financial resources, and many need medical help themselves. In recent years, the United States and other western nations have implemented programs to help educate Tanzanians about HIV and AIDS, and to make drug treatments available to those who need them.

Aside from the terrible toll in human suffering, the spread of AIDS has caused severe economic disruption in Tanzania, which was a poor country to begin with. AIDS has deprived Tanzania of hundreds of thousands of people who would otherwise be contributing productively as part of the labor force. At the same time, the high rate of HIV infection strains the government's already-limited health care resources.

CHANGES AND UNREST

Tanzania's constitution was amended in 1992 to allow more than one political party. The first multiparty elections took place in 1995, when Benjamin Mkapa, a former journalist, was elected. Mkapa's victory at the polls was due largely to his strong stand against corruption and his plans to liberalize Tanzania's economy. But members of a newly formed party, the Civic United Front (CUF), charged election fraud and boycotted the National Assembly for three years before making a truce with Mkapa's CCM. Yet tensions between the two parties persist.

In 1998 Tanzania was the scene of a terrorist attack aimed at the U.S. embassy in Dar es Salaam. On August 7 of that year a powerful truck bomb exploded outside the embassy compound, killing 11 people (8 of them Tanzanians) and wounding more than 70 others. The attack, which coincided with an even deadlier bombing at the U.S. embassy in Nairobi, Kenya, was linked to the Muslim terrorist organization al-Qaeda. Some 30 to 40 percent of Tanzanians are Muslims, but little support for al-Qaeda was expressed; most Tanzanians condemned the attack. For its part, the United States mounted a recovery and relief effort in Tanzania, and the embassy bombing appears to

Benjamin Mkapa served as president of Tanzania from 1995 to 2005.

have had few if any long-term effects on U.S.-Tanzania relations. In March 2003 a new U.S. embassy compound, with heightened security provisions, opened.

In 2000 Mkapa was reelected with more than 71 percent of the vote, but this election was also disputed by the rival CUF, and violent protests ensued. In recent years, some CUF supporters on Zanzibar have demanded more independence for the island, saying that the national union does not represent their interests. In a May 2003 by-election, the CUF earned most of the votes in polling on Pemba Island.

During his two terms as president, Mkapa was praised for implementing painful fiscal reforms and transforming the economy from its socialist origins into one more dependent on free markets. These changes were well received by organizations like the International Monetary Fund (IMF) and the World Bank, and helped to increase foreign investment in Tanzania. Tanzania's economy grew significantly during Mkapa's presidency, while inflation dropped and the country wiped out its foreign debt. However, critics of Mkapa's government complained that, despite the positive statistics, most Tanzanians remained impoverished.

Mkapa retired after two terms as president. In December 2005, Mkapa's foreign minister, Jakaya Mrisho Kikwete, was elected as Tanzania's fourth president. He received 80 percent of the vote. As president, Kikwete continued some of Mkapa's policies, but focused on improving Tanzania's educational system, reducing corruption, and developing Tanzanian industry through new foreign investment.

Over the past decade, Tanzania has taken a leading role in regional peacemaking efforts. During 2002 and 2003, the country hosted peace talks between warring groups in neighboring Burundi aimed at ending that country's civil war. In 2007, President Kikwete helped find a solution to fighting that erupted in Kenya after that country's disputed 2007 election.

Kikwete was re-elected in October 2010 with about 63 percent of the vote. In his second term, the country still faces significant economic and social challenges. These include the high poverty rate, pollution, deforestation, the AIDS crisis, modernization of the electrical grid and infrastructure, and access to education.

Manuvo II, a Tanzanian fishing trawler, steams away from a U.S. Navy warship that had rescued the vessel from pirates. The government reports that from March 2010 to June 2011, there were 27 pirate attacks in Tanzanian waters. "Piracy is a big problem that hits our economy badly," noted President Kikwete, who has asked the United States to provide warships for Tanzania's navy.

The United Republic of Tanzania joins the mainland state Tanganyika with the island state of Zanzibar. (Opposite) The executive branch of Tanzania's government is based in Dar es Salaam. (Right) Zanzibar has its own constitution and government. Here, Amani Abeid Karume (right), president of Zanzibar from 2000 to 2010, meets with United Nations Secretary-General Ban Ki-moon.

3 Two Nations Work Together

THE UNITED REPUBLIC of Tanzania is really two governments in one: it was formed by the union of the sovereign states of Tanganyika and Zanzibar in 1964. Tanzania has two constitutions and two distinct governments.

One constitution applies to the union government, which has authority in matters affecting both the mainland and the island; it came into force in 1977, replacing the 1965 constitution. This constitution now includes all amendments made law since 1995. The other constitution, the Constitution of the Revolutionary Government of Zanzibar of 1979, applies only to Zanzibar and is modeled on the 1977 Union Constitution. It is generally organized in the same way.

The entire country had a one-party political system until 1992, but now there are at least two dozen political parties. Still, the CCM continues to dominate. Its members hold most of the top positions in the government—including the office of president and, as of 2012, the vast majority of seats (268 out of 357) in the National Assembly.

In structure, Tanzania's government, a parliamentary republic, is modeled on the British system and resembles the type of government adopted by many former British colonies. Tanzania's government has three branches: executive, legislative, and judicial.

THE EXECUTIVE BRANCH

The executive branch consists of the president (who is head of state, head of the government, and commander-in-chief of the nation's defense forces), vice president, and council of ministers or cabinet, which includes the prime minister. The president and vice president are elected on the same ballot by popular vote, and each serves a five-year term. No president may serve more than two terms in the union government. The nation's prime minister is appointed by the president from among members of the National Assembly.

The president's office oversees the administration of the country's regions. The president also sets economic policy, which in recent years has largely been directed at attracting foreign investment.

The vice president coordinates union affairs and serves as a link between the government of Tanzania and Zanzibar on non-union affairs. The vice president also oversees environmental policy and works on programs to alleviate poverty.

The prime minister coordinates the activities of all the different cabinet ministries. Each cabinet ministry focuses on a specific branch of the government, such as transportation, agriculture, finance, or foreign affairs. These departments formulate policies, help regulate laws passed on such policies, and provide support services. Cabinet ministers are appointed by the president from among members of the National Assembly. The prime minister is also in charge of the country's emergency preparation and relief efforts, and he supervises the ongoing transfer of the national capital from Dar es Salaam to Dodoma, a process that has been under way since 1973.

In addition to the union government, Zanzibar elects its own president, who serves as head of government for Zanzibar. In December 2010, Dr. Ali Mohamed Shein, a CCM candidate, was elected as the seventh president of Zanzibar. Zanzibar also has its own cabinet ministries.

In 2006, Dr. Asha-Rose Migiro became the first woman to serve in Tanzania's cabinet, holding the post of foreign minister. She later was appointed to a prestigious international post as deputy secretary-general of the United Nations.

THE LEGISLATIVE BRANCH

Tanzania's legislative branch consists of the National Assembly, or Bunge. The Bunge is a *unicameral,* or one-chamber, body (unlike, for example, the United States Congress, which is a two-chamber legislature composed of the Senate and House of Representatives). The Bunge's most important role is to write

Mohamed Gharib Bilal of CCM was elected vice president of Tanzania in 2010. Previously, he served as chief minister of Zanzibar from 1995 to 2000.

and enact laws, but it also authorizes taxes to run the country and operate government programs.

After the 2010 elections, a total of 357 members made up the National Assembly. Of the 357 members, 239 were elected from constituencies, 102 were held by women nominated by the president, and 5 were allotted to members of the Zanzibar House of Representatives. The remainder of the membership was made up by the attorney general and 10 appointments by the president. Bunge members serve five-year terms.

The National Assembly meets in the legislative capital, Dodoma, and many government offices have been transferred, or are in the process of being transferred, there from Dar es Salaam, the former capital. The Bunge holds four sessions each year to propose legislation and create a working budget. Members of the assembly are appointed to various committees that research legislation. The assembly enacts laws that apply to all of Tanzania, as well as laws that apply to the mainland districts.

Zanzibar's House of Representatives proposes and enacts its own laws. The Zanzibar House of Representatives has 50 members. Like their counterparts in the Bunge, they are elected to five-year terms.

THE JUDICIAL SYSTEM

While Tanzania's legal system is based on English common law—a holdover from its days under British rule—it also includes elements of tribal and Islamic law. The five-level judiciary system includes, from lowest court to highest, the primary courts, district courts, resident magistrate courts, High Court, and Court of Appeals. The president appoints the judges of the High Court and Court of Appeals; the chief justice of the Court of Appeals appoints the other judges. All Tanzanian defendants receive legal representation, except for those appearing before the primary courts, whose jurisdiction is limited to minor civil and criminal matters. Tanzania has no trial by jury; decisions on guilt or liability are rendered by judges.

Because of the wide diversity of beliefs and traditions held by the people of Tanzania, the government has developed flexible ways to interpret the law, honor different traditions, and prevent confrontation. Laws that govern personal issues, such as marriage, can be interpreted differently depending on tribal or religious beliefs. For example, Tanzania's Marriage Act of 1971 says that women have to be at least 15 years of age to be married (or 14 under special circumstances). Among certain groups of Tanzanians who traditionally arrange marriages at an earlier age, however, girls may marry at age 12 if their parents consent. Another example is the practice of polygamy, which is still common among some tribes; in this case the law allows men to take more than one wife if the first wife gives her permission.

In Zanzibar, where the majority of the population is Muslim, some laws are based on *Sharia*, an Islamic code of conduct that is considered a basis for law. For example, under Zanzibari law, unmarried women under the age of 21 who become pregnant are subject to two years' imprisonment. In Zanzibar, rulings in Islamic courts can be appealed up to the High Court.

On the mainland, where Muslims do not constitute a majority, Islamic law may still apply to such personal matters as divorce or inheritance if the person is a practicing Muslim. Judges on the mainland have advisers to help them understand Islamic practices in their region, and their decisions can also be appealed to a higher court.

VOTING

All Tanzanians over age 18 can vote, and about 56 percent of the country's population is registered to vote. Before 1992 there was only one party to vote for—the CCM—but political reforms inspired the creation of at least two dozen new political parties. The most prominent of these parties, CHADEMA and CUF, advocate democratic reforms, including laws that protect human rights such as freedom of speech.

CHADEMA traditionally was the less popular of these two opposition parties, winning just four Bunge seats in the 2000 election and five seats in 2005. However, in the 2010 presidential and legislative elections CHADEMA made huge gains. The party's presidential candidate, Willibrod Slaa, received 27 percent of the vote, finishing second and cutting deeply into incumbent President Kikwete's popular vote total (Kikwete's support at the polls dropped by 17 percent from 2005 to 2010). The party also won 44 Bunge seats, making CHADEMA the second-largest party in the National Assembly for the first time.

Although CUF is a national party, most of its support comes from the Zanzibar islands of Unguja and Pemba. As of the 2010 elections, CUF holds 34 seats in the National Assembly, making it the third-largest party in the legislature.

Three other small political parties currently hold a handful of seats in the National Assembly. The National Convention for Construction and Reform (Mageuzi) won four seats, while the Tanzania Labour Party and the United Democratic Party each won a single seat.

Jakaya Kikwete is serving his second term as president of Tanzania.

Elections in Tanzania have often been marred by violence. In Zanzibar, riots by CUF supporters occurred after the 1995 and 2000 elections. In the months leading up to the 2005 election, there were numerous clashes between supporters of CUF and CCM, or involving CUF supporters and police, including one incident in August in which 17 people were injured by police at a CUF rally. Overall, nearly 200 people were wounded in the pre-election violence. After the election, violent protests again broke out on Zanzibar.

Although the October 2010 elections were largely peaceful, in January 2011 four CHADEMA supporters were killed by police while attending a rally in the northern city of Arusha.

(Opposite) Traditional fishing boats, called dhows, float near a Zanzibar beach. Thanks to its spectacular beaches and interesting wildlife, Tanzania has developed a thriving tourist industry. (Right) Women pick tea leaves on a plantation in the Mbeya region of southwest Tanzania. Agriculture an important sector of the country's economy.

4 The Economy: Gains and Setbacks

TANZANIA IS NOT without natural resources, including deposits of gold, diamonds, and the rare gemstone tanzanite. From 2000 through 2008, it possessed one of Africa's fastest-growing economies. Yet Tanzania remains one of the poorest countries in the world, and its people endure a host of social and health problems associated with poverty, including a high infant mortality rate, low life expectancy, and a high illiteracy rate.

Several factors stand in the way of economic development in Tanzania. Much of the workforce is unskilled. The communications system is inadequate, and roads are poor. Despite efforts by the Mkapa and Kikwete administrations to reduce government corruption, the problem remains widespread at the local level. In addition, Tanzania suffers from a heavy debt burden. Since independence, Tanzania has borrowed more than $10 billion from foreign sources.

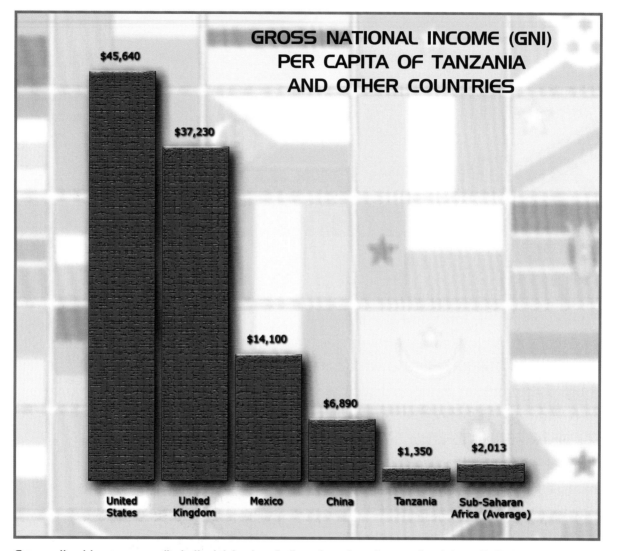

GROSS NATIONAL INCOME (GNI) PER CAPITA OF TANZANIA AND OTHER COUNTRIES

- $45,640 — United States
- $37,230 — United Kingdom
- $14,100 — Mexico
- $6,890 — China
- $1,350 — Tanzania
- $2,013 — Sub-Saharan Africa (Average)

Gross national income per capita is the total value of all goods and services produced domestically in a year, supplemented by income received from abroad, divided by midyear population. The above figures take into account fluctuations in currency exchange rates and differences in inflation rates across global economies, so that an international dollar has the same purchasing power as a U.S. dollar has in the United States.   Source: World Bank, 2011.

Repayment of this debt consumes a large share of the government's annual expenditures, leaving less to spend on programs that might strengthen the Tanzania's economy, including education and job training.

Tanzania's **gross domestic product (GDP)**—the total value of all the goods and services produced within the country—stood at approximately $58.4 billion in 2010. That ranked Tanzania economy 88th out of 227 countries. Nevertheless, since economic reforms began to be implemented by the Mkaba government in the late 1990s Tanzania's economy has grown at an average annual rate of more than 5 percent. Two sectors of the economy are credited with most of that growth: agriculture and tourism.

AGRICULTURE

Agriculture makes up by far the largest sector of Tanzania's economy, accounting for about 40 percent of the GDP, providing about 85 percent of the country's exports, and employing approximately 8 in 10 workers. Yet there is not much good farmland in Tanzania: because of the geography of the land, as well as environmental factors such as declining soil fertility, only about 4 percent of Tanzania's land can be cultivated.

Despite these challenges, the country produces several important crops. The most popular export crops include coffee, cotton, cashews, *sisal*, cloves, and pyrethrum (a species of chrysanthemum that is used to make insect repellent). Food crops include rice, *cassava*, maize (corn), millet, and plantains (which are similar to bananas).

Large tea plantations can be found in the Usambara Mountains of the northeast and around the southern highlands town of Tukuyu. Wheat farms

A young man works on a coconut plantation in rural Zanzibar.

are found in the north, while corn farms are located in the drier areas of the country. Cotton is produced inland from Tanga and Dar es Salaam, along the Rufiji River and as far south as Kilwa. Rice and cotton are grown near Lake Victoria, where sardine fishing is also an important industry. Coffee farms are located around Bukoba and Moshi and near Arusha.

Along the coast, commercial coconut plantations produce *copra*, from which coconut oil and other by-products are made. Cloves, coconut, and spice plantations are found in the Zanzibar archipelago; Pemba is the world's largest producer of cloves. Other spices from Zanzibar include nutmeg, lemon grass, vanilla, and ginger. The islands also have a thriving coastal fishing industry.

Tanzanian livestock ranching has grown steadily over the last few decades. Tanzania now ranks third among African countries in terms of livestock ownership. Cattle account for 75 percent of animals raised in the country, followed by sheep, goats, poultry, and pigs. Most ranching is concentrated in the Arusha and Morogoro administrative regions.

TOURISM

Tourism plays an important role in the Tanzanian economy, accounting for about 8 percent of the GDP. Tourism helps the economy in two ways—it

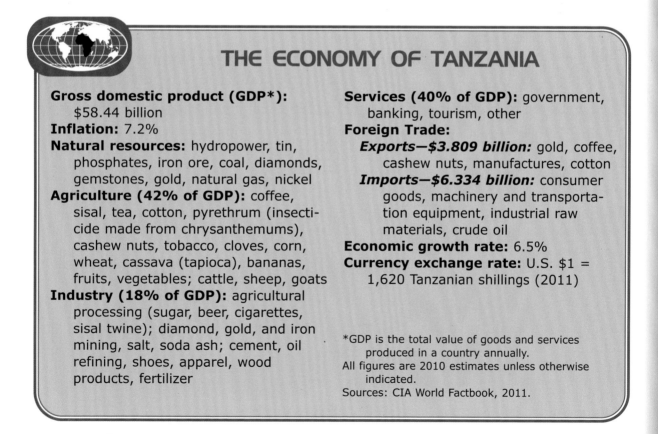

THE ECONOMY OF TANZANIA

Gross domestic product (GDP*):
$58.44 billion

Inflation: 7.2%

Natural resources: hydropower, tin, phosphates, iron ore, coal, diamonds, gemstones, gold, natural gas, nickel

Agriculture (42% of GDP): coffee, sisal, tea, cotton, pyrethrum (insecticide made from chrysanthemums), cashew nuts, tobacco, cloves, corn, wheat, cassava (tapioca), bananas, fruits, vegetables; cattle, sheep, goats

Industry (18% of GDP): agricultural processing (sugar, beer, cigarettes, sisal twine); diamond, gold, and iron mining, salt, soda ash; cement, oil refining, shoes, apparel, wood products, fertilizer

Services (40% of GDP): government, banking, tourism, other

Foreign Trade:
Exports—$3.809 billion: gold, coffee, cashew nuts, manufactures, cotton
Imports—$6.334 billion: consumer goods, machinery and transportation equipment, industrial raw materials, crude oil

Economic growth rate: 6.5%

Currency exchange rate: U.S. $1 = 1,620 Tanzanian shillings (2011)

*GDP is the total value of goods and services produced in a country annually.
All figures are 2010 estimates unless otherwise indicated.
Sources: CIA World Factbook, 2011.

brings money from foreign visitors into the country, and it helps create jobs. Between 750,000 and 1 million tourists visit Tanzania each year, drawn by attractions such as Mount Kilimanjaro, the Ngorongoro Crater, and the beaches of Zanzibar.

Twenty-five percent of Tanzania's land has been set aside for national parks, game reserves, and wildlife management areas, which attracts eco-tourists and adventure vacationers. However, more hotels and personnel trained in the hospitality sector are needed to help the country make the most of its tourism potential.

In recent years, the tourism industry on Zanzibar has suffered from prolonged power outages. Electrical power is currently distributed to the island through an undersea cable from the Tanzanian mainland, which was laid in 1976. In May 2008, the cable was damaged by a power surge, resulting in failure of the electrical grid on Zanzibar. For about a month, the island was dependent on alternative methods of electricity generation (mainly diesel

A safari vehicle passes through national parkland near the Ngorongoro Crater. Most tourists to Tanzania come from the United States, Great Britain, countries of Europe, South Africa, and Kenya.

generators). The power was eventually restored in June 2008, but many of Zanzibar's businesses suffered greatly due to the blackout.

The undersea cable has already exceeded its projected 25-year lifespan by a decade, and the power system remains extremely fragile. In December 2009, a second island-wide blackout occurred in Zanzibar when the cable failed again. This blackout lasted four months, as the power was not restored until March 2010.

MINING AND MANUFACTURING

More than a million ounces of gold are mined in Tanzania each year, and the world's third-largest gold mine is in Arusha. Other mineral resources include nickel in the Kagera Region, iron in the southwest in the Mbeya Region, and gemstones in the Lake Victoria area and in the south near Tunduru.

One of the most prized mineral resources in Tanzania is a gemstone named for the country. Tanzanite is a purple-blue semiprecious stone mined in the hills near Kilimanjaro. It was first discovered in 1967 and is considered rarer than diamonds. The only mine producing these gemstones is southeast of Arusha. Other minerals found in Tanzania include salt, coal, tin, gypsum, and phosphate. By the first years of the 21st century the government had begun exploration and exploitation of natural gas and oil fields.

Tanzanite is a very rare blue/purple gemstone. It is mostly found in the foothills of Mount Kilimanjaro.

Major industries in Tanzania include the processing of sugar, beer, cigarettes, sisal twine, and other agricultural products; oil refining; leatherworking; and the production of cement, textiles, wood products, fertilizer, and salt. Poor roads have hampered manufacturing growth, but in recent years the government has undertaken projects to improve the country's infrastructure.

THE PROBLEM OF POVERTY

By any measure, however, Tanzania is an extremely poor country. The average annual income of Tanzanian families is 33 percent lower than the average of sub-Saharan Africa as a whole. A recent survey found that 36 percent of the population of Tanzania lived in poverty.

High rates of poverty such as those that prevail in Tanzania are associated with other problems. For example, Tanzania's infant mortality rate is high: for every 1,000 Tanzanian babies born, 67 will die before their first birthday. This is one of the highest rates in the world; by comparison, the rate in the United States is about 10 times lower. According to the World Bank, life expectancy in Tanzania in 2011 was just 53 years (compared with about 78 years in the United States and other developed countries).

To reduce poverty, the government has sought international development grants. Since implementing economic reforms during the Mkapa administration, Tanzania has received aid from the World Bank, the International Monetary Fund, the U.S. Agency for International Development (USAID), and other organizations and countries. Both Japan and the United Kingdom, for example, forgave some of Tanzania's national debt, and the Global Fund gave $53 million to fight AIDS, malaria, and tuberculosis.

Residents of Fundo Island, a small islet that is part of Pemba Island, carry a 5,000-liter water cistern to a concrete support pad. The cisterns project will enable the residents of Fundo to have a reliable water source during power outages, which disable the pumps that supply Fundo through a pipeline from the main island of Pemba.

In 2008, the United States awarded Tanzania a $698 million Millenium Challenge Compact grant intended to fund programs that would reduce poverty. The grant—the largest awarded by the U.S. to an African nation—was meant to address Tanzania's critical transportation network needs by improving roads that would increase commerce and help connect communities with markets, schools, and health clinics. Another program covered by the grant is intended to improve the reliability and quality of electric power and extend electricity service to communities not currently served—a vital commodity for rural villages and businesses to thrive. A water project funded by the grant would increase the availability and reliability of potable water for domestic and commercial use. This is expected to increase the health of Tanzanians by reducing the incidence of water-related disease, particularly among children.

(Opposite) The Masai, nomadic cattle herders who roam northern Tanzania and southern Kenya, are perhaps the most famous of Tanzania's 130 tribes. (Right) Arab and Persian influences are readily apparent in Zanzibar, which was ruled by the sultans of Oman for 200 years. These Muslim women are walking on one of Zanzibar's lovely beaches.

5 The People of Tanzania

THREE MAJOR FORCES have contributed to Tanzania's rich cultural heritage: the migration and mingling of various African ethnic groups for 2,000 years; nearly a millennium of Arab influence; and centuries of European rule. These forces helped create a multiethnic, multiracial population with an interesting variety of traditions and customs.

Today, more than 130 distinct ethnic groups call Tanzania home. Ninety-nine percent are native Africans; the other 1 percent consists of Asians, Europeans, and Arabs, living mainly in Zanzibar. On the mainland, 95 percent of the people are of Bantu origin.

The Sukuma tribe from the Lake Victoria area is the largest, with a population of more than 3 million. Other tribes include the Haya, from western Lake Victoria; the Chaga, who live on Kilimanjaro's slopes; the Iraqw, centered near

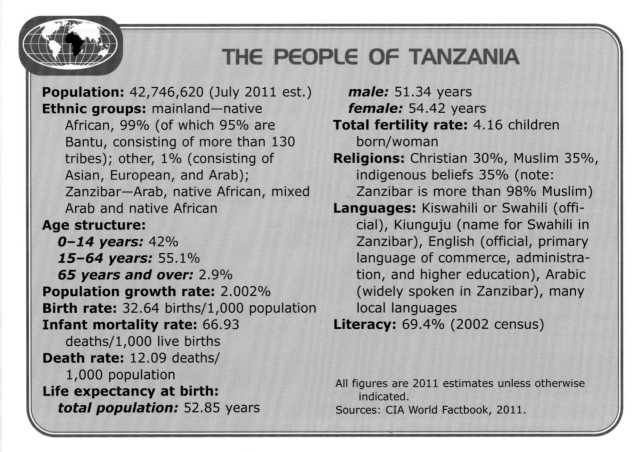

THE PEOPLE OF TANZANIA

Population: 42,746,620 (July 2011 est.)

Ethnic groups: mainland—native African, 99% (of which 95% are Bantu, consisting of more than 130 tribes); other, 1% (consisting of Asian, European, and Arab); Zanzibar—Arab, native African, mixed Arab and native African

Age structure:
  0–14 years: 42%
  15–64 years: 55.1%
  65 years and over: 2.9%

Population growth rate: 2.002%

Birth rate: 32.64 births/1,000 population

Infant mortality rate: 66.93 deaths/1,000 live births

Death rate: 12.09 deaths/ 1,000 population

Life expectancy at birth:
  total population: 52.85 years
  male: 51.34 years
  female: 54.42 years

Total fertility rate: 4.16 children born/woman

Religions: Christian 30%, Muslim 35%, indigenous beliefs 35% (note: Zanzibar is more than 98% Muslim)

Languages: Kiswahili or Swahili (official), Kiunguju (name for Swahili in Zanzibar), English (official, primary language of commerce, administration, and higher education), Arabic (widely spoken in Zanzibar), many local languages

Literacy: 69.4% (2002 census)

All figures are 2011 estimates unless otherwise indicated.
Sources: CIA World Factbook, 2011.

the Great Rift Valley; the Hadza, Nyamwezi, and Gogo in central Tanzania; and the Hehe, Ngoni, and Nyakyusa from the southern highlands.

While the lives of Tanzanian city dwellers are similar to those of urban inhabitants around the world, in certain respects the lifeways of some tribes have not changed much in hundreds of years. For example, the Wa-Chagga live in cone-shaped huts made from thatch and mud. Although they have lived near Kilimanjaro for centuries, they do not want to climb the mountain, believing it full of evil spirits. The Wa-Chagga used to be hunters but are now farmers and sometimes serve as tour guides.

The Iraqw, who live in the Arusha area, reside in cave-style houses on hillsides. Men sleep on one side of these large open homes, women and children on the other.

The Masai, Tanzania's largest non-Bantu group, is perhaps the country's most famous tribe. The Masai call themselves "People of the Cattle" because they are nomadic herders and believe their deity gave them ownership of all the world's cattle. They live across the northern plains of Tanzania and into Kenya. Known as fierce warriors, the tall, thin Masai pierce the arteries of cows to drink their blood, often mixing it with cow's milk. Boys become warriors at the age of 15. Their coming-of-age ceremony traditionally included killing a lion, but that is now illegal.

The tribe that has inhabited the country the longest is probably the Hadza, a migrating tribe of hunter-gatherers who live in groups of about 20 people. They weave round huts from branches and cover them with clay. The Hadza have resisted efforts to limit their living space and have never paid taxes.

The Sandawe people are hunter-gatherers of north-central Africa. Like the Hadza, they speak a click language. They are light skinned, with knotty hair, and their eyelids have the epicanthic fold (like East Asian people) common to the Khoi (also called Bushmen) of South Africa.

In Zanzibar, the island of origin usually determines the tribe a person belongs to. The Waunguja come from Unguja Island, while the Wapemba come from Pemba Island and the Watumbatu from Tumbatu.

LINGUISTIC DIVERSITY

With as many as 120 different spoken languages, Tanzania has the greatest diversity of languages on the African continent. Swahili or Kiswahili is one the country's two official languages (the other is English) and is used in newspapers, textbooks, and literature. There are about 20 dialects, or regional variations.

Scholars trace the use of Swahili back about 2,000 years, when words from different sources were combined with Bantu for trading purposes. For many Tanzanians, Swahili is a second language, learned after a tribal language. Tanzania is home to four major African language families—Bantu, Khoisan (or click language), *Cushitic*, and Nilotic. The click language may have arrived in Tanzania as early as 40,000 years ago with the Hadza. About 1000 B.C. the Cushitic tribes arrived from the Horn of Africa, and about 2,000 years ago Bantu tribes arrived from West Africa.

The largest tribes speaking Bantu languages include the Sukuma, Bena, Chagga, Gogo, Ha, Haya, Hehe, Luguru, Makonde, Makua, Ngoni, Nyakyusa, Nyamwezi, and Nyaturu. The Masai speak a Nilotic language. The Hadza and Sandawe speak Khoisan, and the Iraqw speak a Cushitic language. Arabic is spoken on Zanzibar.

RELIGIONS

Overall, about 35 percent of Tanzanians are Muslims, with Christians constituting about 30 percent of the population. Of the remaining Tanzanians, most practice traditional tribal religions. The population of Zanzibar is almost

One of many mosques in Dar es Salaam.

completely Muslim. There are also small communities of Hindus, Sikhs, and Zoroastrians.

Many tribes worship ancient spirits. For example, the Masai worship the god Engai and his messiah, Kindong'oi. Some tribes worship the baobob tree, a forest, the sun, or their ancestors. Practicing Muslims or Christians may also observe some traditional *animistic* beliefs and occasionally consult traditional healers.

The spires of St. Joseph's Cathedral, a Roman Catholic church, rise above the rooftops of Stone Town, Zanzibar. The church was built by French missionaries in the 1890s; it is a popular tourist attraction and is still in use today.

EDUCATION

Tanzania's education system is loosely modeled on that of Great Britain. There are seven years of primary school and four years of secondary school, with two more years of preparation for university.

Primary school is free, but the cost of buying school uniforms and other supplies can make it difficult, if not impossible, for some children to attend. More than half of all students receive a primary school education, but only about 5 percent enroll in the secondary level. Girls make up only one-fourth of the students who graduate from secondary school.

Under the leadership of Julius Nyerere, Tanzania achieved one of the highest literacy rates in Africa, but have been declining since the 1980s. By 2000, just 57 percent of Tanzanian children were enrolled in primary school.

That year, the Tanzanian government set a goal of enrolling all school-age children in the school system by 2015. The government reduced or eliminated fees that parents were expected to pay toward education in 2002, and that helped to boost the enrollment rate. By 2010, the government was reporting that about 97 percent of school-age children were attending Tanzanian schools.

Unfortunately, while the student population has grown, the effectiveness of Tanzania's educational system is in question. Thousands of new schools have been constructed under the Kikwete administration, but these facilities are often underutilized because of shortages of trained teachers and a lack of educational supplies. The debt-burdened government has little money to spend on teachers' salaries and school supplies. Some schools have no textbooks or desks. The charity ActionAid estimates that class sizes in

Tanzanian children hold packets of school supplies at the Tongoni Primary School in Tanga.

Tanzania have risen to one teacher for every 53 students; a "good quality learning environment" should have no less than one teacher for 40 students. The student-to-teacher ratio is even worse in rural areas, sometimes approaching 75 or 100 students to one teacher.

WOMEN'S ROLES

Even after years of socialist rule, under which the government strove to achieve equality in the treatment of men and women, Tanzanian women continue to receive less education and play less of a role in politics than do men. This probably has much to do with attitudes rooted in centuries of male-dominated tribal organization.

In the rural areas of Tanzania, women do most of the work involved in rearing children, keeping house, raising crops, and getting water. Despite

A Tanzanian woman quarries stone at a mine in Shinyanga, Tanzania. Women can earn about a dollar a day with their labor; for many, it is the only opportunity to feed their families

government condemnation, some tribes still practice female circumcision when girls reach puberty. In some parts of Tanzania, girls are considered ready for marriage when they reach their early teens.

TANZANIAN ART

Art in Tanzania has a long history—dating back to the Stone Age, in fact. On the walls of caves, Stone Age artists depicted scenes of hunting and dancing, using natural pigments mixed with animal fat.

More recently, the 20th-century Tanzanian artist Edward Said Tingatinga created bold, bright paintings featuring cartoon-like birds, animals, and fish on vivid patterns. Tanzania's most famous artist inspired many African painters to use bicycle paint to create their own colorful works of art, called Tingatinga painting.

Tanzanian crafts include weaving, tie dying, pottery, and printed fabrics. One type of colorful printed wrap worn by Tanzanian women is called the *kanga*. The fabrics often contain a proverb or riddle. A similar garment, but without the proverb or riddle, is the *kitenge*, which is made of thicker cloth.

The Makonde people are known for their fanciful wood, ebony, and ivory carvings. Their *ujamaa* carvings look like totem poles. These "trees of life" include carvings of people and animal figures, often reaching several feet in length.

Some of Tanzania's most famous wood carvings are the elaborate doors found on Zanzibari homes and palaces. There are said to be 560 such doors in Stone Town, the oldest dating back to 1700. Favorite themes include the lotus flower, fish, dates, and frankincense.

(Opposite) A crowded market near Arusha, one of Tanzania's largest cities. (Right) Stone Town, as the old part of Zanzibar City is called, is a city of prominent historical and artistic importance in East Africa. Its architecture reflects the diverse influences underlying the Zanzibari culture, blending Arab, Persian, Indian, African, and European elements.

6 Along the Caravan Route and the Coast

MANY OF TANZANIA'S most important cities were ancient trading centers or stops on centuries-old caravan routes. Some of the more prominent cities are Arusha, Bagamoyo, Dar es Salaam, Dodoma, Iringa, Morogoro, Mwanza, Tanga, and Zanzibar City.

ARUSHA

Arusha Municipality, the capital of the Arusha Region, had an estimated population of about 1.2 million, according to the most recent census. Its residents are a mix of nationalities and backgrounds and include the WaArusha, the area's original inhabitants. The town, which lies on the southern slopes of Mount Meru at an altitude of 4,757 feet (1,450 meters), boasts impressive views of Mount Kilimanjaro. The altitude ensures a temperate climate even though the town is close to the equator.

Blessed by fertile volcanic soils and two rainy seasons, the area is an agricultural center. Coffee, maize, wheat, bean, fresh flower, and banana farms surround Mount Meru. Cattle are kept on the rich grasslands.

Once a German garrison town, Arusha is now gateway to the world-famous national parks and conservation areas of Tanzania—Serengeti, Ngorongoro, and Mount Kilimanjaro. Arusha National Park, a 30-minute drive from the town, is a favorite tourist destination for viewing butterflies, birds, baboons, and monkeys. Hundreds of thousands of tourists visit this region every year.

BAGAMOYO

Bagamoyo, in northeastern Tanzania, was once one of the most important *dhow* ports along the East African coast, shipping slaves, ivory, salt, and copra to Zanzibar and beyond. The name of the town is said to come from the Swahili word for "throw down your heart," since it was the point of no return for slaves who were probably leaving Africa forever. After the end of the slave trade, Bagamoyo became a way station for European explorers and missionaries traveling to the interior, and from 1887 to 1891, it was the capital of German East Africa.

Though its population today is less than 50,000, Bagamoyo is still an important boat building and fishing center. It is also home to the Chuo ca Sanaa, Tanzania's largest arts college, which teaches dancing, drama, music, and painting.

Dar es Salaam remains Tanzania's largest and most important city.

DAR ES SALAAM

The vibrant city of Dar es Salaam was the official national capital of Tanzania until 1973, when the government designated Dodoma the new capital. However, some government offices remain in Dar es Salaam pending the completion of the transfer to Dodoma.

The bustling metropolis that is today Tanzania's largest city (estimated population: 2.5 million) grew up on the site of a small fishing village called Mzizima. It was renamed Dar es Salaam, which means "haven of peace," in 1866 by Sultan Seyyid Majid of Zanzibar.

Dar es Salaam has a busy harbor and an international airport. Its colorful markets sell food, spices, pottery, shells, carpets, silver, brass, and textiles.

The city also offers an interesting mix of African, German, Asian, and British architecture. Some of Tanzania's most beautiful beaches—palm fringed and with white sand—can be found to the south of the city.

DODOMA

The name of Tanzania's official legislative capital city derives from the word *Idodomya*, or "place of sinking," which legend says refers to an elephant having sunk in a nearby swamp. A stop along the 19th-century caravan route, Dodoma became a city in 1907 under German colonial rule. With the advent of the railway, Dodoma evolved into an important mission center. When the British took control of the region after World War I, they made Dodoma their provincial headquarters.

Dodoma is not nearly as large as the former capital—its has a population of about 325,000—but it lies near the geographic center of the country, and that is the reason President Julius Nyerere decided, in 1973, that it should be the nation's capital. While most of the legislative offices have moved to Dodoma, many administrative offices are still located in Dar es Salaam.

The Dodoma area is home to the Gogo people, accomplished farmers who have succeeded in cultivating crops there despite a lack of rain. The area's sandy soil yields groundnuts, maize, millet, beans, and grapes for a fledgling wine industry.

IRINGA

Iringa, which overlooks the Little Ruaha River, lies in the middle of Tanzania's tea-growing region. A district capital, it claimed an estimated 2004 population of nearly 113,000. Iringa is known for its German and African architecture and for its proximity to the Ismila Stone Age Site, which contains some of the most important Stone Age finds ever identified.

Another nearby tourist attraction is Ruaha National Park, the country's second-largest national park. The park is home to more than 8,000 elephants and almost 500 species of birds. The region is favored by hikers because of its breathtaking views. It is also home to many baobab trees, which are said to live up to 1,000 years.

Zebras at a water hole, Mikumi National Park. Visitors to Mikumi frequently stay in the regional capital of Morogoro, which is nearby.

MOROGORO

Morogoro (estimated 2004 population: 234,000) is a regional capital located near the foot of the Uluguru Mountains. The Morogoro region is one of Tanzania's most important agricultural areas, producing sisal, coffee, sugarcane, yams, citrus fruits, and livestock. Another local industry is tobacco processing.

Morogoro, which lies 120 miles (200 km) west of Dar es Salaam, has become a popular weekend destination for Dar es Salaam residents and for visitors traveling to Udzungwa National Park and Mikumi National Park.

MWANZA

Mwanza, the most important port on Lake Victoria and the second-largest urban area in Tanzania, had an estimated 2004 population of 400,000. The municipality is growing so fast, however, that inadequate housing has become a serious social and environmental problem. Mwanza's economy centers on fishing, agriculture, and related activities. It is also a trading center for nearby gold and diamond mines.

Tourists visit this area to see its smooth granite rock formations, which are known as koppies. The most distinctive is Bismarck Rock, a pointy formation that seems to stand guard over the ferry harbor. The town is known for its panoramic waterfront view of Lake Victoria. It's also close to Rubondo Island National Park, a haven for nature lovers who want to view its wildlife, including crocodiles, hippos, and elephants. The Sukuma, who live in the area, are Tanzania's largest tribe.

TANGA

Tanga, a port city and regional capital in northeastern Tanzania, is connected by rail to the interior, making it an important commercial, industrial, and transportation center. In 2004 it had an estimated population of more than 220,000. Tanga's exports include sisal, cotton, tea, and coffee. Manufactured goods include rolled steel, plywood, clothing, and twine.

During the period of European exploration, Tanga served as a base for caravans into the African interior. The city is known for its beautiful beaches to the south and its vibrant night life. The Amani Botanical Gardens are located west of Tanga.

ZANZIBAR CITY

Zanzibar City, located on the island of Zanzibar (or Unguja), is separated from the mainland by about 22 miles (35 km) and is six degrees south of the equator. The city of about a quarter million residents is known for its fascinating history, picture-perfect beaches, and distinctive architecture, including palaces, Persian baths, forts, and carved wooden doors.

Zanzibar Island was once the world's largest producer of cloves. Cloves remain an important crop, along with coconut products and spices, but tourism is a growing industry. Visitors from around the world come to attend the annual Zanzibar International Film Festival, also known as the Festival of the Dhow Countries.

A CALENDAR OF TANZANIAN FESTIVALS

Tanzanians observe a variety of national as well as religious holidays. Certain Christian observances, such as **Good Friday** and **Easter Sunday**, and Muslim festivals, such as **Eid al-Fitr** and **Eid al-Kabir**, are based on a lunar calendar, so their dates vary from year to year.

January

January 1, **New Year's Day**, has only officially been a holiday in Tanzania since the early 1990s. Some Tanzanians believe that if you are sleeping when the year turns, you may have bad luck and could "sleep all year." So, like many people around the world, Tanzanians celebrate through the stroke of midnight. Members of the Chagga tribe travel to the place of their ancestors on New Year's Day.

January 12 is celebrated as **Zanzibar Revolution Day**.

February

February 5 is **CCM Foundation Day**, commemorating the founding of the Chama Cha Mapinduzi. Tanzania's dominant political party was created in 1977, with the merger of the mainland party TANU with Zanzibar's Afro-Shirazi Party.

April

On April 26, **Union/Labor Day** commemorates the unification of Zanzibar and Tanganyika in 1964.

May

Worker's Day, also known as **International Labor Day** or **Mei Mosi**, takes place on May 1. In the cities, the day is marked with parades. People also celebrate by singing, dancing, writing poems, and playing games. Money is given to the poor and the sick.

July

July 7 is **Saba Saba** (literally, "seven seven") **Day**, which commemorates the founding of the Tanganyika African National Union. The Saba Saba Fair includes everything from cars to handicrafts and refreshments. Celebrations can last up to a week.

The **Zanzibar International Film Festival** takes place in July and is the largest cultural festival in East Africa for world music and films from Africa, India, and the Middle East. Two other festivals in Zanzibar in July are the **Mwakakongwa and Tamasha Festivals**, showcasing traditional music and dance.

In parts of the islands of Zanzibar and Pemba, **Mwaka Koga** or **Nairuz**, the Zoroastrian

A CALENDAR OF TANZANIAN FESTIVALS

New Year, is celebrated around the third week in July. During the **Shirazi Makunduchi New Year** festival, its date set by a pre-Islamic solar calendar, men challenge their enemies of the past year by waving banana leaves. The men fight and make up while women sing around them. They set a house of spirits on fire to symbolize the banishment of the previous year's troubles. Then there's lots of feasting, drinking, and dancing.

August

August 8 is **Peasants Day** or **Farmer's Day**, also known as **Nane Nane**. On this day farmers gather to sell their crops, and there is an abundance of cheap, delicious food to buy and eat.

August 26, **Sultan's Day**, is celebrated only in Zanzibar.

September

September 1 is celebrated as **Heroes Day**, honoring current members of Tanzania's defense forces as well as those who died fighting colonialism.

October

October 14 is **Mwalimu Nyerere Day**, named after former president Julius Nyerere. It is also the last day of the **Uhuru Torch Race**. This torch was first lit on Mount Kilimanjaro in 1961. It is lit in a different part of Tanzania each year and carried during the race. The torch symbolizes the love and mutual respect that can conquer hatred.

October 29 is **Naming Day**, the day that Tanganyika and Zanzibar officially changed their name to the Republic of Tanzania.

December

December 9 is **Tanzanian Independence/ Republic Day**. Also known as **Siku ya Uhuru**, the day celebrates Tanganyika's independence from British rule in 1961.

On December 25 Tanzanians celebrate **Christmas** (or **Krismasi**). Christian Tanzanians attend services and spend the day with family and friends, feasting, singing, and dancing. Christians often share a Christmas Day feast with Muslim friends.

RECIPES

Mandhazi **(Coconut Bread from Zanzibar)**

(Serves 4)
4 cups all-purpose flour
1 cup sugar
1 tin coconut milk
1 Tbsp. oil
1 tsp. yeast
2 tsp. cardamom seeds (from the cardamom pod)
Water

Directions:
1. Mix yeast with a pinch of sugar in a quarter cup of warm water.
2. Mix other dry ingredients, then add yeast mixture, coconut milk, and enough water to make dough.
3. Roll out dough and cut into interesting shapes.
4. Deep-fry until golden brown in color, or bake in oven at 350°F for 10 to 15 minutes.

Mandhazi, Coconut Bean Stew, and Cassava with Chicken recipes adapted from Bea Sandler, *The African Cookbook.* New York: Carol Publishing Group, 1993.

Coconut Beans Stew from Zanzibar

(Serves 4)
2 tins pigeon peas (green) or black-eyed beans
1 tin coconut milk
1 fresh tomato, cut into 8 pieces
1 cup water
1 tsp. ginger and garlic paste
1 tsp. curry powder
1/2 tsp. salt
Fresh coriander leaves / cilantro

Directions:
1. In a saucepan, combine coconut milk, water, spices, and pigeon peas or black-eyed beans.
2. Add tomato pieces.
3. Cook on low heat until gravy is thick.
4. Serve with chopped coriander and rice or whole wheat pita bread.

Cassava with Chicken

(Serves 4)
1 small packet cassava
7 oz. chicken breast without skin
1 tin coconut milk
2 medium-sized tomatoes, diced
2 sticks cinnamon
2 cardamom pods
2 cloves garlic
1 medium-sized onion, chopped
1 Tbsp. cooking oil
1/2 tsp. curry powder
1 lemon
Salt to taste
Water

Directions:
1. Boil the cassava until cooked. Drain the water and mash the cassava.
2. In a medium-sized saucepan, heat some oil at medium temperature and add the cinnamon, garlic, tomatoes, and cardamom pods. Then add the chopped onion and fry until brown.
3. Add curry powder and fry the mixture for another minute.
4. Add the chicken and a little water and let it cook. When the curry is ready, mix with the mashed cassava, adding two cups of water and the coconut milk. Mix well.
5. Cook until the mixture thickens. Serve hot.

Supa Ya Kuku (Chicken Soup)

(Serves 8)
1/2 cup onions, finely chopped
1/2 cup cabbage, finely chopped
1 small tomato, diced
1 stalk celery, finely chopped
2 oz. butter or margarine
5-lb. Cornish game hen, quartered
2 quarts water
1 tsp. salt
1/2 tsp. pepper

Directions:
1. Sauté onions, cabbage, tomato, and celery in the butter or margarine.
2. Put water in a large pot and add game hen and salt and pepper to the water. Simmer gently for an hour until meat is tender.
3. Remove the bird, and cut 1 cup of meat in half-inch cubes.
4. Add meat cubes and sautéed vegetables to the soup and simmer for another half hour.

GLOSSARY

ambergris—a waxy substance, believed to originate in whale intestines, that is used as a fixative in perfumes.

animistic—characterized by the belief that spirits inhabit inanimate objects and natural phenomena; characterized by the belief that spirits exist apart from bodies.

archipelago—a chain of islands.

Bantu—a family of languages spoken in central and southern Africa, or a member of an African people speaking any of these languages.

cassava—any of several plants having a fleshy root stock that yields a nutritious starch; also called tapioca root.

click-tongue language—any of a number of Khoisan languages that include many clicking sounds and that are spoken by the Hottentot, Sandawe, and Hadsa tribes.

copra—dried coconut meat, used to produce coconut oil and other by-products.

Cushitic—originating in the northeastern regions of Africa, particularly Ethiopia and Somalia; a language family in Tanzania.

dhow—a sailing vessel used especially by Arab traders.

gross domestic product (GDP)—the total value of goods and services produced within a country in a one-year period.

hominid—a member of a family of primates that includes modern humans as well as extinct ancestors.

moorland—treeless, usually bog-filled land.

one-party state—a state in which there is only one political party.

plateau—a relatively flat section of land at elevation.

Shirazi—originating in or characteristic of a region in Persia (modern-day Iran).

sisal—a durable fiber used for twine and rugs.

sultan—a Muslim ruler.

unicameral—characteristic of a lawmaking body with a single legislative chamber.

Zoroastrian—a follower of Zoroastrianism, a religion founded in Persia in the sixth century B.C. by the prophet Zoroaster.

PROJECT AND REPORT IDEAS

Topographic Map

Illustrate the contrast in land heights between Tanzania's lowlands and mountainous areas by making a map that shows surface features. Using clay or a flour and salt mixture, create and label the following features:

- Major mountain peaks, such as Mount Kilimanjaro and Mount Meru.
- Important cities, such as Arusha, Dodoma, Dar es Salaam, Mwanza, and Zanzibar City.
- Rivers and lakes, including the Great Ruaha River, Lake Victoria, and Lake Tanganyika.
- Wildlife conservation areas, such as the Serengeti National Park, the Selous Game Reserve, and the Ngorongoro Crater Conservation Area.
- Regions such as the mainland central plateau, the highlands, the coastal area, and the Zanzibar archipelago.

Cross-Curricular Reports

Write one-page, five-paragraph reports answering any of the following questions. Begin with a paragraph of introduction. Then write three paragraphs, each developing one main idea. End with a conclusion that summarizes your topic.

- What can be done to protect Tanzania's endangered species?
- Why is the poverty level in Tanzania so high?
- How well did the reforms of Julius Nyerere's government work?
- How effective has the introduction of more than one political party been?
- What role can wealthy countries such as the United States play in helping Tanzania and other African nations fight diseases such as malaria and AIDS?

PROJECT AND REPORT IDEAS

Oral Presentation

Research and prepare a five-minute oral presentation on any of the following topics. Make sure to incorporate photos or other visual aids to help your presentation come alive.

- The diversity of wildlife in Tanzania
- Growing tourism
- Mount Kilimanjaro
- The Masai
- The changing role of women in Tanzania
- The merging of cultures in Tanzania
- Zanzibar
- Jane Goodall's chimpanzees
- European explorers in Africa
- Islam in Tanzania

Experience the Culture

- Create and share a Tanzanian dish.
- Listen to and share music from Tanzania.
- Learn a Tanzanian dance.
- Learn some phrases of Swahili with a partner and stage a conversation.

CHRONOLOGY

ca. 3000 B.C.	Egyptian traders arrive on the eastern African coast.
ca. A.D. 750	Persian or Shirazi Muslims migrate to the area, as do Persian followers of the ancient Zoroastrian faith.
1498	Portuguese explorer Vasco da Gama lands on Zanzibar while charting a route to the Orient around Africa and through the Indian Ocean.
1502	Portugal begins attacking coastal cities; within five years the Portuguese have control over the entire coastal area and its trade.
1698	The people of Zanzibar, with help from Omani Arabs, drive out the Portuguese; Omani sultans begin ruling Zanzibar.
1841	Sultan Sayyid Said of Oman moves his capital from Oman to Zanzibar.
1856	Explorers Richard Burton and John Speke go to Tanganyika to search for the source of the Nile River.
1858	Speke finds Lake Victoria and names it after the queen of England.
1884	Karl Peters of the Society for German Colonization signs treaties with tribal chiefs in Tanganyika, bringing the area under German control.
1890	The Anglo-German Agreement is signed on November 1, giving Germany control over Tanganyika and declaring Zanzibar a British protectorate.
1897	The British abolish slavery on Zanzibar.
1905	The Maji Maji Rebellion begins.
1921	The League of Nations gives Britain the mandate to administer Tanganyika.
1929	The Tanganyika African National Union (TANU) is formed.
1946	The United Nations declares Tanzania a U.N. Trust Territory.
1954	Julius Nyerere becomes the leader of TANU.
1960	Free elections are held for 71 seats in the Tanganyika Legislative Council; TANU wins all but one seat and Nyerere becomes chief minister.
1961	Tanganyikan independence is proclaimed on December 9.

1962	Tanganyika adopts a constitution and Nyerere is elected president.
1963	The British create the independent Sultanate of Zanzibar on December 10.
1964	On April 26 Zanzibar and Tanganyika merge to form a single country that is later named the United Republic of Tanzania.
1977	TANU and the Afro-Shirazi Party merge into the Chama Cha Mapinduzi.
1985	Nyerere resigns; Ali Hassan Mwinyi becomes president of Tanzania.
1992	Tanzania's Union Constitution is amended to allow for more than one party; more than a dozen political parties are soon formed.
1995	Benjamin Mkapa of the CCM is elected president in Tanzania's first multi-party elections; members of the opposition Civic United Front (CUF) stage violent protests, claiming election fraud.
2000	Mkapa is reelected amid more charges of election tampering.
2001	In January, Tanzanian police crack down on CUF supporters agitating for new elections, killing at least 30 people.
2005	Jakaya Kikwete of CCM is elected president with 80 percent of the vote.
2006	Zanzibari and Tanzanian governments clash over the island's failure to ratify the 2001 Human Rights and Good Governance Convention.
2008	In February, Mizengo Pinda becomes prime minister of Tanzania.
2010	The Convention on International Trade in Endangered Species of Wild Fauna and Flora (CITES) rejects Tanzania's request to sell elephant ivory on the world market; in October, President Kikwete is elected to a second term.
2011	In January, four CHADEMA supporters attending a rally in Arusha are killed by Tanzanian police.
2012	In April, the African Development Bank Group announced that the Tanzanian government will receive a $216 million loan for road construction projects in eastern and southern Tanzania.

FURTHER READING/INTERNET RESOURCES

Briggs, Philip. *Tanzania, Zanzibar, Pemba, and Mafia.* 6th ed. Chalfont St. Peter, England: Bradt Travel Guides, 2009.

Finke, Jens. *Rough Guide to Tanzania.* New York: Rough Guides, 2010.

Fitzpatrick, Mary, Natalie Folster, and David Lukas. *Lonely Planet Tanzania.* Victoria, Australia: Lonely Planet Publications, 2008.

Winks, Quintin. *Tanzania—Culture Smart!: The Essential Guide to Customs and Culture.* New York: Random House, 2009.

Salkeld, Audrey. *Kilimanjaro: To the Roof of Africa.* Washington, D.C.: National Geographic, 2002.

Travel Information

http://www.tanzaniatouristboard.com
http://www.zanzibartourism.net
http://www.africatravelresource.com

History and Geography

http://www.Tanzania.go.tz
http://www.tanzaniaodyssey.com

Economic and Political Information

https://www.cia.gov/library/publications/the-world-factbook/geos/tz.html
http://www.africanet.com

Culture and Festivals

http://zanzibar.net
http://www.lonelyplanet.com/tanzania/

FOR MORE INFORMATION

Embassy of the United Republic of Tanzania
1232 22nd Street NW
Washington, DC 20037
Phone: 202) 884-1080
Fax: (202) 797-7408
Email: ubalozi@tanzaniaembassy-us.org
Website: www.tanzaniaembassy-us.org

U.S. Department of State (travel advisories)
2201 C St. NW
Washington, DC 20520
Phone: (202) 647-5225
Fax: (202) 647-3000

Tanzania High Commission
205 E. 42nd St.
New York, NY 10017
Phone: (212) 972-9160

Tanzania Tourism Board
IPS Building
Third Floor
P.O. Box 2485
Dar es Salaam, Tanzania
Phone: (+51) 27672/3
Fax: (+51) 46780
e-mail: safari@ud.co.tz
Website: www.tanzaniatouristboard.com.

INDEX

Afro-Shirazi Party, 30
   See also political parties
agriculture, *47*, 49–51
   See also economy
AIDS, *34*, 35–36, 55
Almeida, Francisco de, 25
Amani Botanical Gardens, 73
Anglo-German Agreement of 1890, 27
Angola, 33
area, 11–12, 16
arts, 64–65
   See also culture
Arusha, 67–68
Arusha National Park, *67*, 68
Azania, 22

Bagamoyo, 68–69
Bantu tribe, 22, 57–58, 60
   See also tribes
Barghash (Sultan), 27
Bunge. *See* National Assembly
   (Bunge)
Burton, Richard, 25

Chama Cha Mapinduzi (CCM), 30,
   36–37, 39–40, 44–45
   See also political parties
Civic United Front (CUF), 36, 37, 44,
   45
   See also political parties
climate, 16, 17–18
colonialism (European), 23–28
culture, 57–65

Dar es Salaam, 37, 41–42, 45, *67*, 69,
   70
Dodoma, 41–42, 69, 70

economy, 32–33, 35, 47–55
education, 31, 33, 62–63
England, 26–28, 30, *61*

festivals, 74–75

Gama, Vasco da, 23–25
gender roles, 63
geographic features, 11–17
Germany, 26–28, *61*
Gombe National Park, 14–15
Goodall, Jane, 14–15
government, 34, 36–37, 39–43, 44–45,
   55
    See also political parties
Great Rift Valley, 12
gross national income, 48

Hadza tribe, 58, 59, 60
   See also tribes
health care, 35–36
   See also AIDS
history, 21–34

Idi Amin, 33
industry and services, 51, 52–53
   See also economy
Iraqw tribe, 57, 59, 60
   See also tribes
Iringa, 70–71
Islam. *See* religion
Ismila Stone Age Site, 71
Karume, Abeid Amani (Sheikh), 30
Khalid (Sultan), 27
Kilimanjaro (Mount), *11*, 13, 16, 18,
   52, 68
Kilwa Kisiwani, 23, 24–25

Kiunguju (Swahili). *See* language

Lake Malawi (Lake Nyasa), 15
Lake Tanganyika, 14, 25
Lake Victoria, 14, *15*, 26, 72
language, 21, 22–23, 31, 58, 60
League of Nations, 27–28
Leakey, Louis and Mary, 14
legal system, 42–44
Livingstone, David, *24*, 25, 26

Maji Maji Rebellion, 27
Majid, Seyyid (Sultan), 69
Marriage Act of 1971, 42–43
Masai Steppe, 13
Masai tribe, *57*, 59, 60
   See also tribes
Mikumi National Park, *71*, 72
Mkapa, Benjamin, 36, 37, 40, 44–45
Morogoro, *71*, 72
Mount Kilimanjaro, *11*, 13, 16, 18, 52,
   68
Mount Meru, 13, *67*, 68
Mozambique, 33
Mwanza, 72
Mwinyi, Ali Hassan, 34
Mzizima, 69
   See also Dar es Salaam

National Assembly (Bunge), 41–42,
   44–45
    See also government
natural resources, 47, 51, 52
Ndayizeye, Domitien, *36*
Ngorongoro Crater Conservation
   Area, 14, 19, 52, 68
Nile River, 14, *15*, 25–26

Numbers in **bold italic** refer to captions.

Nyerere, Julius, *21*, 29, 30–34, 63, 70

Olduvai Gorge, 14, 21
Omani Arabs, 22, 23, 25, 58
    See also tribes

Pemba Island, 16, 37
People's Rebulic of Zanzibar and
    Pemba, 30
    See also Zanzibar islands
Peters, Karl, 26
political parties, 29, 30, 33, 36–37,
    39–40, 44–45
    See also government
population, *32*, 49, 54, 58, 67, 69, 70,
    72, 73
Portugal, 23–25, *61*
poverty, 53–55

al-Qaeda, 37

refugees, 32, 54
religion, 22, 23, 42–44, 45, 58, 60–62
Rhodesia, 33
Ruaha National Park, 71
Rubondo Island National Park, 72

Sandawe tribe, 59, 60
    See also tribes
Selous Game Reserve, 15–16
Serengeti National Park, *11*, *12*,
    13–14, 68
Serengeti Plain, 13
Sharia (Islamic law), *43*, 44
    See also legal system
Sheba, 22
Speke, John Hanning, 25–26

Stanley, Henry Morton, *24*, 25, 26
Stone Town, Zanzibar, 17, *57*, 65
bin Sultan, Sayyid Said, 25
Sultanate of Zanzibar, 30
    See also Zanzibar islands
Swahili (Kiswahili). *See* language

Tanga, 73
Tanganyika, 11, 18
    government, 39
    history, 21, 25, 26–29
        See also Tanzania; Zanzibar
        islands
Tanganyika African National Union
    (TANU), 29, 30
        See also political parties
Tanzania
    area, 11–12, 16
    cities, 67–73
    climate, 16, 17–18
    culture, 57–65
    economy, 32–33, 35, 47–55
    education, 31, 33, 62–63
    founding of, as the United
        Republic of Tanzania, 21, 30, 39
    geographic features, 11–17
    government, 34, 36–37, 39–43,
        44–45, 55
    health care, 35–36
    history, 21–34
    independence, 28–30
    legal system, 42–44
    natural resources, 47, 51, 52
    population, *32*, 49, 54, 58, 67, 69,
        70, 72, 73
    wildlife, *11*, *12*, 13–14, 16, 18–19, 71
tanzanite, 47, 52

terrorism, 37
Tingatinga, Edward Said, 64
tourism, 51–52, 71, 72
    See also economy
trade, 22, 23
tribes, 21–22, 31, 57–61
Tumbatu Island, 16

Udzungwa National Park, 72
Uganda, 33, 35
ujamma, 31–33
United Nations, 28
United Republic of Tanzania. *See*
    Tanzania

voting, 44–45

Wa-Chagga tribe, 58–59
    See also tribes
wildlife, *11*, *12*, 13–14, 16, 18–19, 71

Zanzibar House of Representatives,
    42, 45
Zanzibar Island (Unguja), 16–17, 73
Zanzibar islands, 11, 16–17, 18, 37,
    50, 52, 57, 59
    government, 39, 41–42, 45
    history, 21–23, 24–25, 27, 30
    legal system, 43–44
        See also Tanganyika; Tanzania
Zanzibar City, 73

CONTRIBUTORS/PICTURE CREDITS

Professor Robert I. Rotberg is Director of the Program on Intrastate Conflict and Conflict Resolution at the Kennedy School, Harvard University, and President of the World Peace Foundation. He is the author of a number of books and articles on Africa, including *A Political History of Tropical Africa* and *Ending Autocracy, Enabling Democracy: The Tribulations of Southern Africa*.

Joan Vos MacDonald is the author of *The Ultimate Baby Book, Tobacco and Nicotine Drug Dangers*, and *Cybersafety*. She has written for newspapers and magazines on a variety of subjects.